North Riverside Public Library District
2400 S. Des Plaines Avenue
North Riverside, IL 60546
708-447-0869
www.northriversidelibrary.org

FOOTBALL'S G.O.A.T.

JIM BROWN, TOM BRADY, AND MORE

JOE LEVIT

Lerner Publications ◆ Minneapolis

Lerner Publications Company
A division of Lerner Publishing Group, Inc.
241 First Avenue North
Minneapolis, MN 55401 USA

For reading levels and more information, look up this title at www.lernerbooks.com.

Main body text set in Aptifer Sans LT Pro.
Typeface provided by Linotype AG.

Library of Congress Cataloging-in-Publication Data

Names: Levit, Joseph, author.
Title: Football's G.O.A.T. : Jim Brown, Tom Brady, and more / Joe Levit.
Other titles: Football's Greatest Of All Time
Description: Minneapolis, Minnesota : Lerner Publications Company, [2019] | Series: Sports' Greatest Of All Time | Includes bibliographical references and index.
Identifiers: LCCN 2018035854 (print) | LCCN 2019001835 (ebook) | ISBN 9781541556362 (eb pdf) | ISBN 9781541556027 (library binding : alk. paper)
Subjects: LCSH: Football players—United States—Biography—Juvenile literature. | Football players—United States—Rating of—Juvenile literature. | National Football League—History—Juvenile literature.
Classification: LCC GV939.A1 (ebook) | LCC GV939.A1 L469 2019 (print) | DDC 796.3320922 [B] —dc23

LC record available at https://lccn.loc.gov/2018035854

Manufactured in the United States of America
2-48598-43474-10/10/2019

CONTENTS

In 1967, the Green Bay Packers beat the Kansas City Chiefs in the first Super Bowl, 35–10.

KICKOFF!

National Football League (NFL) fans love to talk about the game's greatest of all time (G.O.A.T.). But have you ever tried to make a list of the best players in the history of the NFL? It's a tough task. How can fans compare players in different eras? The game has changed so much over the years.

FACTS AT A GLANCE

JIM BROWN'S career rushing average of 104.3 yards per game is the best in NFL history. He's held the record for more than 50 years.

LAWRENCE TAYLOR is one of just two defensive players to win the league's Most Valuable Player (MVP) award.

BARRY SANDERS rushed for more than 1,500 yards in four straight seasons.

TOM BRADY led the New England Patriots to the two greatest comebacks in Super Bowl history.

The NFL didn't allow African Americans to play in the league between 1933 and 1946. That means some of the best players were banned because of the color of their skin. In 1967, 16 teams competed to play in the first Super Bowl. By 2002, the league had grown to 32 teams. The length of the season rose too. It went from 14 games in 1967 to 16 games in 1978. More teams and games meant more players got the chance to rack up amazing stats.

In football, the quarterback is often the star of the team. Quarterbacks begin most plays with the ball in their hands. That gives them a lot of control over each play. Players at other positions stand out in different ways. They break through tackles or chase down ballcarriers. The greatest of all time play at a high level for many years.

The average NFL career lasts just a few years, but great players, such as Tom Brady, sometimes play much longer.

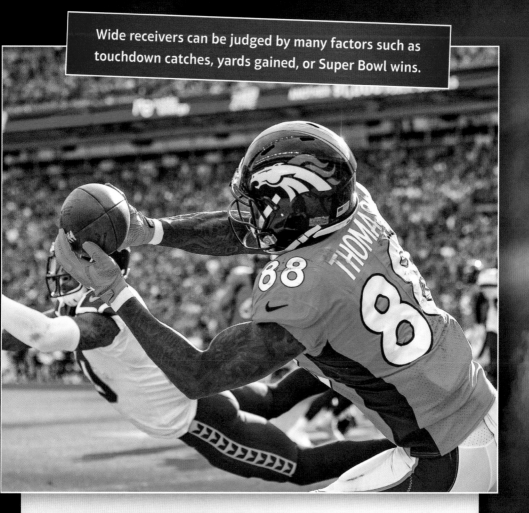

Wide receivers can be judged by many factors such as touchdown catches, yards gained, or Super Bowl wins.

You may not know all the names in this book. You may disagree with the order of the players. Or you may feel as if someone important was left out. Amazing players like Walter Payton, Johnny Unitas, and Dick Butkus missed the cut. Your friends will have their own opinions too. It's okay to disagree. Thinking about great NFL players and forming your own opinions about them is what this book is all about.

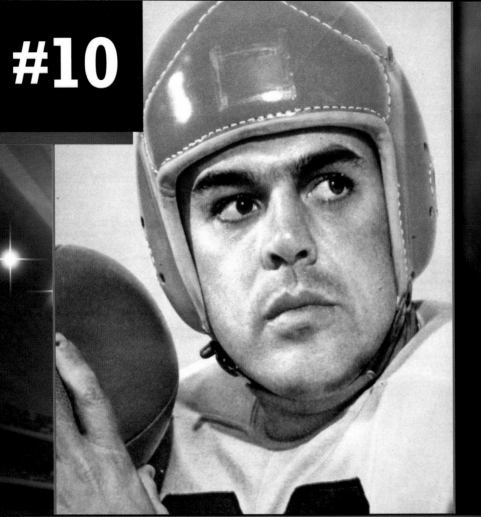

OTTO GRAHAM

Stats and awards are two ways to measure greatness. But they don't tell the whole story. Winning is what matters most at football's top level. Quarterback Otto Graham played for the Cleveland Browns from 1946 to 1955. During that time, Graham made Cleveland a winner.

The Browns played in the All-America Football Conference from 1946 to 1949. Graham led the Browns to a championship at the end of each of those seasons. In 1948, Cleveland had a perfect 15–0 record.

The Browns joined the NFL in 1950. Many fans thought the NFL was a tougher league. But the Browns won the NFL Championship in their first year. Graham passed for 298 yards and four touchdowns in the title game. He also rushed for 99 yards. He led Cleveland back to the championship game in each of the next five years. The Browns won two of those contests.

OTTO GRAHAM STATS

▶ His career winning percentage of .788 is the best for a quarterback.

▶ He holds the **NFL** career record with nine yards gained per pass attempt.

▶ He played in his league's championship game every season of his 10-year career.

▶ He was First Team All-Pro seven times.

▶ He was a member of the NFL's 75th Anniversary All-Time Team.

JOE MONTANA

Few quarterbacks have been as successful on the game's
biggest stage as Joe Montana. His teammates called him
Joe Cool. That's because he performed best in the biggest
moments.

Montana led the San Francisco 49ers to the playoffs
after the 1981 season. They faced the Dallas Cowboys,

and the winner would go to the Super Bowl. Losing in the fourth quarter, he marched his team down the field with time running out. Then he sealed the win with a six-yard toss to the back of the end zone. Wide receiver Dwight Clark leaped and made a grab that fans call the Catch. The famous play sent the 49ers to the Super Bowl for the first time.

In 1989, the 49ers and Montana were in the Super Bowl for the third time. They were losing to the Cincinnati Bengals in the fourth quarter 16–13. Montana led his team on a 92-yard touchdown drive with just over three minutes left. His heroics helped the 49ers win 20–16.

JOE MONTANA STATS

- He was First Team All-Pro three times.

- He won the **NFL MVP** award in **1989** and **1990**.

- He won four **Super Bowls** and three **Super Bowl MVP** awards.

- He threw 122 **Super Bowl passes** without an interception.

- He's one of two players in **NFL history** to throw two touchdown passes of at least 95 yards.

#8

ANTHONY MUNOZ

Anthony Munoz was the best player on the Bengals offensive line for years. He had amazing quickness and strength. He kept himself in great shape. Munoz would go on long runs every day. So much running is rare for offensive linemen. They usually focus on lifting weights instead. Running helped Munoz stay on the field and rarely miss a game.

Munoz was great at keeping defenders away from his quarterback. Defenders would sometimes rush right at him. But he was big and strong enough to hold his ground at the line of scrimmage. Other times, a defender would try to run around him. But Munoz would simply push the defender right past the quarterback. Munoz was so good at his job that teammates and coaches called him the Eraser. He erased defenders from the play. Munoz helped Cincinnati reach two Super Bowls. They lost both games to the 49ers.

ANTHONY MUNOZ STATS

- He was a member of the NFL's 75th Anniversary All-Time Team.

- He was the first longtime Cincinnati Bengals player elected to the Pro Football Hall of Fame.

- He scored four touchdowns in his career, a rare feat for an offensive lineman.

- He was voted the best offensive lineman in the NFL in 1981, 1987, and 1988.

- He was First Team All-Pro nine times.

DON HUTSON

Don Hutson played for the Green Bay Packers from 1935 to 1945. He invented routes as a wide receiver that players still use in the NFL. Modern rules prevent defenders from blocking receivers five yards past the line of scrimmage. But when Hutson played, defenders could shove and grab receivers anywhere on the field. That makes his stats even more impressive. Hutson was the team's kicker too. He also played defense.

He had an amazing season in 1940. He led the NFL in touchdown catches with seven and interceptions with six! Two years later, he may have been even better. Hutson caught 74 passes for 1,211 yards. No one else in the league caught more than 27 passes that year or had half as many yards. He also scored 17 touchdowns in just 11 games.

DON HUTSON STATS

▶ He was voted First Team All-Pro eight times.

▶ For 44 years, his 99 career touchdown catches were the most in NFL history.

▶ He scored a record 29 points in a single quarter in 1945. He scored four touchdowns and kicked five extra points.

▶ He won the NFL MVP award in 1941 and 1942.

▶ He was a member of the NFL's 75th Anniversary All-Time Team.

BARRY SANDERS

Barry Sanders was a unique running back. He could quickly change directions or spin past defenders. That helped him break out with long runs. He never carried his team to a Super Bowl. But he did help the Detroit Lions reach the playoffs in 1991. His 47-yard touchdown run capped Detroit's 38–6 win over the Dallas Cowboys. The victory is Detroit's only playoff win in the last 60 years.

Sanders set an NFL record in 1997 of 14 straight games with more than 100 rushing yards. He rushed for exactly 2,000 yards in those games. He was just the second player ever to gain 2,000 yards in 14 games.

Sanders decided to retire after 10 seasons in the league. He finished his career with 15,269 rushing yards. Sanders averaged 1,526 yards per year. At that pace, he would have beaten Walter Payton's all-time rushing record if Sanders had played just one more season.

BARRY SANDERS STATS

▶ He was First Team All-Pro six times.

▶ His career average of 99.8 rushing yards per game is second best in NFL history.

▶ He twice won the Offensive Player of the Year award.

▶ He broke an NFL record with at least 1,500 rushing yards in four straight seasons.

▶ He was the first running back with at least 1,500 rushing yards in five seasons.

JIM BROWN

Sports fans think of Jim Brown as one of the greatest athletes in US history. He's a member of the Pro Football Hall of Fame and the College Football Hall of Fame. He's also in the US Lacrosse Hall of Fame. He was an avid lacrosse player in college. Brown helped the Cleveland Browns win the NFL Championship in 1964. And he set the NFL record for career rushing yards. That record stood for 19 years.

Brown was a big, strong running back. He could bowl defenders over when he wanted to. He could also run right past them. His amazing balance and quickness helped him break into the open for long runs. Brown's career average was 104.3 rushing yards per game. That's the best average ever. He was also tough. He didn't miss a single game in his career. After retiring at the age of 29, Brown began acting. He also worked to promote civil rights in the United States.

JIM BROWN STATS

► He was First Team All-Pro eight times.

► He led the league in rushing in eight of his nine NFL seasons, including five seasons in a row.

► He won the NFL MVP award three times.

► He won the Rookie of the Year and MVP awards in the same season.

► He was a member of the NFL's 75th Anniversary All-Time Team.

LAWRENCE TAYLOR

Lawrence Taylor joined the New York Giants in 1981. From the beginning, he was an amazing force on the football field. He played linebacker like no other player. Taylor refused to wait for running backs to sprint his way. He blasted through offensive lines to hunt runners behind the line of scrimmage. And he sacked quarterbacks with

Taylor had matchless skills on the field. He was extremely fast for his size. He was also one of the strongest players in the league. He could run around the offensive line on one play. Then on the next play, he might shove a lineman right back into the quarterback for a sack. His aggressive style was also a strength. Taylor often played as if he wanted to win more than the other team did. He helped the Giants win the Super Bowl in 1987 and 1991.

LAWRENCE TAYLOR STATS

▶ Taylor was First Team All-Pro eight times.

▶ He was a three-time Defensive Player of the Year winner.

▶ He recorded 20.5 sacks in 1986, making him one of just eight players ever with more than 20 sacks in a season.

▶ He was a member of the NFL's 75th Anniversary All-Time Team.

▶ He won the NFL MVP award in 1986. Only two defensive players have ever won the award.

REGGIE WHITE

Reggie White was a natural athlete. Unlike most defensive linemen, he rarely lifted weights early in his career. But he was still extremely strong. White joined the Philadelphia Eagles in 1985. Opposing teams often used two offensive linemen to try to slow him down. It usually didn't help. White had at least eight sacks in each season he played. He twice led the NFL in sacks.

White became a member of the Green Bay Packers in 1993. He greatly improved the team's defense. In 1997, White helped the Packers reach the Super Bowl. He dominated the New England Patriots in the game. White set a Super Bowl record with three sacks. His amazing play helped secure a 35–21 victory for the Packers. White finished his career as the all-time sack leader for the Eagles, the Packers, and the NFL.

REGGIE WHITE STATS

► He was First Team All-Pro eight times.

► He won the **Defensive Player of the Year** award in 1987 and 1998.

► He was a member of the NFL's 75th Anniversary All-Time Team.

► He recorded 21 sacks in just 12 games in 1987.

► With the Eagles, White recorded 124 sacks in

JERRY RICE

Wide receiver Jerry Rice played with Hall of Fame quarterbacks Joe Montana and Steve Young. But Rice's hard work made him a success in the NFL. He pushed himself all the time. Rice sprinted up hills in the off-season to stay in shape. During the season, no one prepared for games more than he did. His hard work carried him to three Super Bowl victories.

Rice was a superstar for 20 NFL seasons. In 1987, he caught 22 touchdown passes to set a new NFL record. The record stood for 20 years. He scored 15 or more touchdowns in five different seasons. He played so well for so long that some of his records will never be broken. He logged 22,895 yards receiving in his career. That's nearly 7,000 yards ahead of the next closest player. His 208 career touchdowns are 33 more than anyone else has scored.

JERRY RICE STATS

▶ He was First Team All-Pro 10 times.

▶ He won the Offensive Player of the Year award in 1987 and 1993.

▶ He played in 29 playoff games, the third most of all-time.

▶ He gained 215 receiving yards in the 1989 Super Bowl, a record for the championship game.

▶ He was a member of the NFL's 75th Anniversary All-Time Team.

TOM BRADY

Tom Brady is among the all-time leaders in almost every important stats category for quarterbacks. He has performed like an MVP for almost 20 years. But Brady's most important stats reflect his team success. He's won more than three times as many NFL games as he's lost. Brady has led the New England Patriots to the Super Bowl eight times. That's three more times than any other quarterback.

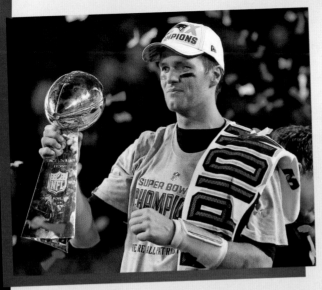

Brady led two of the biggest comebacks in Super Bowl history. He was 10 points down against the Seattle Seahawks in 2015. Seattle had one of the best defenses ever. But Brady guided his team to a 28–24 victory.

Brady outdid himself two years later against the Atlanta Falcons. He overcame a 25-point Falcons lead to win in overtime. No other team has ever come from more than 10 points behind to win a Super Bowl.

TOM BRADY STATS

▶ He was First Team All-Pro three times.

▶ He won five Super Bowls.

▶ His 196 regular-season wins and 27 playoff wins are the most in NFL history.

▶ He passed for 505 yards in the 2018 Super Bowl, the most ever in the title game.

▶ He passed for 28 touchdowns and two interceptions in 2016. No quarterback in NFL history had ever thrown so many touchdowns with so few interceptions.

YOUR G.O.A.T.

IT'S YOUR TURN TO MAKE A G.O.A.T. LIST ABOUT THE NFL. Start by doing some research. Think about the rankings in this book. Then check the Further Information section on page 31. You'll find books and websites that can tell you more about football players of the past and present. Try searching online for more information. Or you can check with a librarian, who may have other resources. You might even try reaching out to NFL players and teams to see what they think.

Once you're ready, make your list of the greatest players of all time. Then ask your friends to make their own lists and compare them. Do you have players that no one else listed? Are you missing anybody that your friends think is important? Talk it over. Then try to convince them that your list is the **G.O.A.T.!**

FOOTBALL FACTS

► It took 34 years for the New Orleans Saints to earn their first playoff win.

► Only one NFL team has scored three touchdowns in less than a minute. The New England Patriots scored three times in 51 seconds against the New York Jets in 2012. In 2014, New England scored three times against the Chicago Bears in 57 seconds.

► Quarterback Brett Favre set an NFL record with 297 games played in a row.

► Some footballs used to be made of pig bladders. That's why footballs are called pigskins. Modern footballs are made of cowhides or rubber. One cowhide is enough material for about 10 footballs.

► A 1967 game in Green Bay, Wisconsin, was so cold that fans call it the Ice Bowl. But the coldest game in league history may have been the Freezer Bowl in Cincinnati, Ohio, in 1982. With the wind whipping briskly, the temperature on the field felt like −59°F (−51°C).

GLOSSARY

civil rights: rights granted to citizens by the government, such as the rights to vote and own property

First Team All-Pro: one of the best players in the NFL according to votes by sports media members

interception: a play in which a defender catches a forward pass

linebacker: a defender who usually plays behind the line of scrimmage

line of scrimmage: an imaginary line that marks the position of the ball at the start of each play

NFL's 75th Anniversary All-Time Team: a list of the greatest players in NFL history chosen by media members and league officials in 1994

offensive line: the five players on the offensive side of the line of scrimmage who block defenders

route: a path that a receiver runs during a play to try to get open to make a catch

sack: to tackle the quarterback behind the line of scrimmage

winning percentage: games won divided by the total number of games played

FURTHER INFORMATION

Braun, Eric. *Tom Brady*. Minneapolis: Lerner Publications, 2017.

Jacobs, Greg. *The Everything Kids' Football Book: All-Time Greats, Legendary Teams, and Today's Favorite Players—with Tips on Playing like a Pro*. Avon, MA: Adams Media, 2016.

NFL FLAG Football
https://nflflag.com

NFL—Play 60
http://www.nfl.com/play60

Savage, Jeff. *Football Super Stats*. Minneapolis: Lerner Publications, 2018.

Sports Illustrated Kids—Football
https://www.sikids.com/football

INDEX

PHOTO ACKNOWLEDGMENTS

Image credits: Focus on Sport/Getty Images, pp. 4, 10, 11 (bottom), 16, 17 (bottom), 18, 19, 22, 23 (bottom), 25 (bottom); Jim Davis/The Boston Globe/Getty Images, pp. 6, 23 (top); Dustin Bradford/Getty Images, p. 7; AP Photo/NFL Photos, p. 8; Bettmann/Getty Images, p. 9; AP Photo/Mark Duncan, p. 11 (top); AP Photo/Paul Spinelli, p. 12; AP Photo/David Durochik, p. 13; AP Photo/John Lindsay, p. 14; AP Photo/Pro Football Hall of Fame, p. 15 (top); Bruce Bennett Studios/Getty Images, p. 15 (bottom); Allen Kee/Getty Images, p. 17 (top); John F. Grieshop/Getty Images, p. 20; Nate Fine/Getty Images, p. 21 (top); Allen Dean Steele/Getty Images, p. 21 (bottom); Joseph Patronite/Getty Images, p. 24; AP Photo/Lennox McLendon, p. 25 (top); Doug Murray/Icon Sportswire/Getty Images, p. 26; Rob Carr/Getty Images, p. 27 (top); Barry Chin/The Boston Globe/Getty Images, p. 27 (bottom); Mtsaride/Shutterstock.com, p. 28. Design elements: EFKS/Shutterstock.com; Iscatel/Shutterstock.com; conrado/Shutterstock.com; DinoZ/Shutterstock.com.

Cover: Patrick Smith/Getty Images (Tom Brady); Focus on Sport/Getty Images (Jim Brown); EFKS/Shutterstock.com (stadium background); Iscatel/Shutterstock.com (design element).